KITTENS in

Shinkansen

Japan's super-fast Shinkansen, or "Bullet Train," which zooms at speeds of over 200 km/hour, was inaugurated in 1964 along Japan's Tokaido region, connecting Tokyo with Osaka, the business center of western Japan. Today's Tokaido Shinkansen makes the 552.6-km (345.4-mile) run in less than three hours. More recent lines include the Sanyo Shinkansen, between Osaka and Hakata; the Tohoku Shinkansen, connecting Tokyo and Morioka; and the Joetsu Shinkansen, linking Tokyo and Niigata. There have been no injuries involving the Shinkansen in its nearly three decades of operation.

Mikoshi

The *mikoshi* is a portable shrine used to carry local deities during annual festivals throughout Japan. This wooden structure consists of a platform on which rests the deity's "house," its walls and roof ornately decorated with brass, the figure of a phoenix often placed at the apex. To the bottom of the *mikoshi* are attached two long wooden poles, by which numerous traditionally-clad revelers carry the shrine on their shoulders. The *mikoshi* appears in ancient records as far back as A.D. 749, when Todai-ji, the temple of the Great Buddha, was built in Nara.

Masks of Okame and Hyottoko

Okame, known for her homely features, is loved and respected as a bringer of good fortune.

Hyottoko, who is forever blowing out a flame, is revered as the god of fire, the god of the wind, and even the god of blacksmithing. Both of these popular masks are often used for playful games.

Decorated "Bear-Claw" Bamboo Rake

The teeth of this bamboo rake are curled over like the claws of a bear, and fastened together in the shape of a fan. Originally a farming tool, it has come to be regarded as one which is used to "rake in" good fortune. These rakes are sold at Tokyo's famous Ohtori Shrine every November.

Tai Yaki

These cakes, stuffed with sweet bean jam and grilled in the shape of a *tai*, or sea bream, are sold during festivals and other local celebrations. Since the sound of *tai* rhymes with *medetai*, which means "happy," the sea bream is traditionally considered an omen of good luck.

Beckoning Cat

According to ancient Chinese literature, when a cat rubbed its face with its forepaw its master could expect visitors. Over the ages the "beckoning cat" has thus come to be regarded as an omen of good luck for proprietors of shops. White cats, made of either porcelain or papier-mache and painted in bright colors, are often found facing the entrance of stores, inns, restaurants and other establishments throughout Japan.

Bangasa

The *bangasa* originated as a crude type of umbrella among Osaka's merchant class at the beginning of the eighteenth century. At that time it was made by coating bamboo with oil, then splitting the bamboo into 30 to 35 "ribs," which were covered with paper. The more elegant, modern version of the *bangasa*, consisting of fifty ribs, is dyed and decorated with colorful string.

Geta

In ancient times *geta*, or wooden clogs, were a symbol of authority. From around the seventh century the slightly elevated footware came to be used to prevent the hem line at the bottom of the kimono from getting dirty when drawing water, washing clothes or crouching.

In the eighteenth century, *geta* first became popular among the common people. With the Westernization of the late 1800's came the popularization of shoes, and today *geta* are generally worn only with traditional Japanese clothing.

Noren

Noren are short, split curtains hung at the entrance to shops, restaurants and other establishments to indicate they are open for business. Originally used to keep out sunlight and dust (perhaps as far back as the twelfth century), *noren* became widely popular about four hundred years ago.

Traditionally made of cotton or linen, *noren* are usually white, dark blue, light brown or pale yellow. As the word *noren* can also refer to a shop's good reputation, when an apprentice of a shop opens his own establishment he might be honored with the *noren* of his former master.

Soba

Soba, or buckwheat noodles, first appeared in Japan in the mid-seventeenth century, when they were peddled mostly at night. In the eighteenth century restaurants specializing in soba began to appear, popularizing these noodles.

There are two basic ways of eating soba: either the boiled noodles are allowed to cool, sometimes topped with thin strips of dried laver and dipped into a special sauce; or they are added to a hot broth, accompanied by tempura, eggs, boiled fish cake, fried tofu or other ingredients.

Tempura

This typical Japanese dish was actually introduced to Japan by the Portuguese in the late sixteenth century. Tempura consists of small pieces of fish, shrimp, squid, shellfish and vegetables, dipped into a batter of flour, eggs and water, then deep fried in refined vegetable oil. The cooking time is about 4 or 5 minutes, after which the hot tempura is dipped into a sauce made of soup broth, soy sauce and sweet rice wine, and garnished with grated white radish and ginger.

Tokyo Metropolitan Government Office

The futuristic Tokyo Metropolitan Government Office, the nation's tallest structure, was completed in Tokyo's Shinjuku district in March 1991, at a total cost of 156.9 billion yen (over one billion dollars). Equipped with state-of-the-art technology, this "intelligent" building faces a 5,000-square-meter public plaza featuring its own stage. A panoramic view of the city is afforded from the 45th floor, which is only a one-minute elevator ride from ground level.

Straw-Covered Sake Cask

In olden times straw mats were laid out for purification rites. It is for this reason that casks of Japanese sake, wrapped in straw, are traditionally given as gifts during festivals and other celebrations.

Nishikigoi Carp

Traditionally this ornamental carp, named for its brilliant colors and gorgeous pattern, has been kept in garden ponds for the sake of its beauty. Since olden times carp have been taken from their natural habitat to beautify the mountain ponds of Niigata Prefecture. Nowadays, *nishikigoi* are also bred in such prefectures as Fukushima, Saitama and Hiroshima.

Hot Spring

The Japanese archipelago, situated in a volcanic region, is consequently blessed with an abundance of hot springs. Long ago hot springs mainly served their local villages, but nowadays these baths, renowned for their medicinal, rehabilitative and therapeutic effects, attract people from far and wide.

Paper Balloon
Made from sheets of brightly colored paper, this toy balloon is inflated through a small hole. Like its counterpart in the West, it has long been a favorite among Japanese children.

Bamboo
Bamboo, of which there are a thousand different kinds, has a wide variety of uses, including food, tools and building materials. Tea ceremony utensils, practice fencing swords and flutes are made from bamboo. Bamboo sprouts, which appear at the beginning of spring, are a popular delicacy. Depending on the kind of bamboo, sprouts may grow up to 120 cm (four feet) per day, reaching adulthood in just two or three months.

Thatched Roof
While pampas grass and reeds are used as feed for cows and horses, they also serve a more aesthetic, but no less practical purpose. Construction of the thatched roofs of traditional Japanese farmhouses requires a large quantity of these grasses, and plenty of labor. It is for these reasons that these grasses have traditionally been grown by local people, who also construct the roofs of their village farmhouses.

Temple Bell

While the bronze bell of the Buddhist temple has traditionally been used to ring out the time of day and call people to assembly, its resonant sound symbolizes sanctity and purity. The temple bell, along with Buddhism, was introduced to Japan from China in the sixth century. Japan's oldest temple bell, dating from A.D. 698, is housed at Myoshin-ji temple in Kyoto.

It is said that when a temple bell is struck on its side with a special wooden hammer, the resonance thus produced brings the surrounding people to their senses, converts them to Buddhism and offers them paradise.

Calligraphy

Calligraphy was developed in Japan and China, countries where Chinese characters, or *kanji* are used. By the ninth century Japanese nobles, who held in great esteem the culture of China's Tang Dynasty, placed great educational importance in the practice of calligraphy. The invention of the indigenous Japanese characters in the ninth century furthered the development of calligraphy, which takes its place along with literature and painting at the pinnacle of Japanese cultural tradition. Writing brushes, Chinese ink, paper and inkstone are the implements used in calligraphy.

Hibachi

The hibachi, once the typical source of heat in the Japanese home, has become a rarity in modern days. Its heat comes from pieces of burning charcoal, placed atop ashes which usually fill about two thirds of the hibachi. These braziers are generally made of ceramic, wood or metal.

Japanese Sweets
Many of these sweets are Japanized versions of recipes imported from China and Europe before the seventeenth century. Traditionally enjoyed with green tea, Japanese sweets vary in color and shape according to the season of the year.

Origami
The making of different figures by folding—but never cutting—a single piece of paper is a distinctive Japanese art form. *Origami* is believed to have been brought to other cultures by Japanese entertainers traveling overseas. Among the most popular *origami* figures are cranes, dolls, ships, insects and animals.

Flower Cards
This is a game in which a deck of forty-eight colorful flower cards is used, four for each month of the year, with each month represented by one of twelve flowers or plants. Flower cards are believed to have originated in the mid-eighteenth century, but were often banned as a form of gambling. With the introduction of regular playing cards into Japan in the mid-nineteenth century, the ban was lifted from flower cards, and by the end of the century the game was extremely popular.

**Japan's super-fast Shinkansen, or Bullet Train, zooms at speeds
of over 200 kilometers an hour.**

**Portable shrines, called *mikoshi*, are used to carry deities though
the streets during local festivals throughout Japan.**

The smiling mask of Okame, bringer of good fortune, and that of Hyottoko, always blowing out a flame, are often used in traditional celebrations.

This bamboo rake, reputed to help its owner gather in wealth, can be purchased at Tokyo's Ohtori Shrine every November.

Tai Yaki (grilled hot cakes filled with sweet bean jam) are shaped like a good luck fish, the *tai* (sea bream), which is reputed to bring happiness (*medetai*).

The beckoning cat, often seen in Japanese storefronts, is thought to wave in customers.

The familiar *bangasa* is a colorful umbrella traditionally made by splitting a bamboo stalk into ribs, then attaching brightly dyed paper.

Wooden clogs, or *geta*, are still used in Japan when wearing traditional clothes on rainy days.

Noren are short, split curtains that are hung at the entrance of a Japanese shop or restaurant to indicate that it is open for business.

Buckwheat noodles, known as soba, are delicious dipped into a cold sauce, or eaten with hot broth and garnishes.

Tempura, deep fried fish and vegetables dipped into a light sauce, was introduced into Japan from Portugal in the late sixteenth century.

Tokyo's futuristic Metropolitan Government Office building, completed in 1991, features a panoramic view of the city from the 45th floor.

Casks of Japanese rice wine, or sake, are traditional gifts at celebrations.

Specially bred ornamental carp, called *nishikigoi*, are often found in Japanese garden ponds.

Volcanic hot springs are to be found throughout Japan, attracting visitors from far and wide for their healthful benefits.

Traditional Japanese balloons are made from sheets of brightly colored paper, and inflated through a small hole.

There are more than a thousand different varieties of bamboo in Japan, used for everything from construction, to eating utensils, to food.

Grasses and reeds are especially grown in Japan as materials for constructing thatched roofs for traditional farmhouses.

Ringing the bronze bell in a Japanese Buddhist temple is reputed to bring those who hear it closer to paradise.

The artistic rendering of Japanese characters ranks with literature and painting at the pinnacle of Japanese cultural tradition.

The hibachi, or charcoal brazier, was once the typical source of heat in a Japanese home.

Beautiful and delicious Japanese sweets are traditionally enjoyed with astringent green tea. They vary in color, shape, and ingredients with the seasons.

Origami, or Japanese paper folding, often features animals and birds, like the crane.

Flower cards are both beautiful and fun to play with. Players try to match them.